*

SHADOW CATCHING

Poems of Existential Peering

Brad Dehler

TROIKA STUDIOS & PUBLISHNG
SALEM, OREGON

*

Shadow Catching: Poems of Existential Peering

Printed in the United States of America
1st edition

Additional copies are available at
Barnes and Noble // Books-A-Million
Booktopia.com.au // Ebay // Thriftbooks
Abebooks.com // Goodreads.com // WritersCafe
Betterworldbooks.com // Duckscottage.com
or www.Amazon.com

For product information, permission to use material from this text, or further permissions questions- please e-mail to:
Troika7@gmail.com

A special thanks to the formatters at CreateSpace
and to the details, content, and quality reviewers from Kindle Direct Publishing KDP
A Book of Bard; Poemadeh candidate

ISBN-13: 978-0-9829733-6-3
Hardcover ISBN: 978-0-9829733-7-0

Troika Studios & Publishing; Salem, Oregon
Printing by KDP/CreateSpace; Charlotte, South Carolina
An Amazon Company
USA

*

"The book "Syzygy" written by Brad Dehler is almost thirty years of lessons, thoughts, questions and learning to understand the meaning of being alive. The poetry reflects the movement of our world. Sometimes we understand and sometimes, we do not. Some of the poetry is brutally honest and some of the poetry is gentle and kind. The writer takes us on a ride grasping at hope, his books plunge you to many places and into many lessons. You must read again to catch the hidden wisdom. I recommend the books- which are to be re-read, to find solid ground in complexity."

- **John Castellenas "Coyote": Michigan Poet.** Published by Poetry Soup, Short-Edition, Poem Hunter, Writer's Café, among other sources.

"I like this poetry of Brad Dehler. No mean feat to write so incisively and succinctly. Intricate and lyrical. Brilliant."

-Davey Payne: Poet of Dumfries, Scotland

"Speechless. Amazing, great poetry. "We are the shore of something great" > amazing wisdom within such imagery. Really good poetry.... genuine, direct and concise- with perfect sense of math and metric. I humbly bow, sincerely."

-Amber Stone: Nepali-English Poet; "Just a loving work in progress", Poetry 101 Member

*

*

INTRODUCTION
Shadow Catching

Shadow Catching is the fourth book written by Brad Dehler; proceeding the books Cantus, Dose & Syzygy. Syzygy was released in the year 2020 when Brad Dehler asserted that it was a year of 'clear vision' prior to the start of the year. It was not foreseen how apropos this notion was in considering how our eyes have opened up to the overreach of those in power. Dose is the second book (the "dos" book written) which explores art and poetry as medicine (as in a dose of medicine). Cantus is aptly named as the initial song, initial book as it was projecting this inspired style of poetry. In reference of Troika Studios and Publishng, the troika represents that unfailing driving force before, during and after most difficult challenges. While at the same time, a trifecta as the avenue for success.

The title of this book: 'Shadow Catching', refers to Brad's Indian name bestowed upon him by his late beloved grandmother Lilly who taught about his ancestors, history and Sioux native ways. Ancestors who have since been relegated to Rosebud Reservation in particular and other surrounding reservations.

This book is an example of how a few mysteries may be deciphered from the world around us. A way of hunting and trapping some enigmas. While some poems are complete puzzles to be identified and appreciated (in this book Shadow Catching), some

are individual pieces with puzzle edges showing-
there is more to explore. These are to further
thought processing and discussion in an open-ended
fashion. In addressing how these poems arise; it
seems as an inspiration, divine spark sent for
perspective and ultimately a development of
obligation and relation to Truth.

These poems float solo, not part of a larger
constructed story and not for personal
aggrandizement. Sometimes serious of nature, at other
times in levity. Promote these with patience in your
own thoughts. Perhaps there are solutions & may they
be helpful to you. There is potential to elevate some
prayerfully; if so- would be so blessed by you.

This is an attempt to share the goodness in
publishing these poems. I am not claiming to be a
master of it. It is more of the "what is to be done"
and not so much the "how" until the reader processes.
Why? It is for you to decipher.
The who is you, I, us.

*

*

Shadow Catching
Table of Contents

*

*

*

*

*

Bloodlines
Lay down talk of quantums
Back to Running Bull
    Still running
Sitting Bull
    Still sitting
Red Cloud
    Still elevating
We share the same blood
Oneness
Like the connection
Of vehicle and bridge
Different material
In the same cause
Cross over, we track it
Or the same pause
Arrow to target

                Salem 09.13.21

*

Trenches carved
     By our walk
Forming our path
     Warming our expectation
The trenches we dig
     Devise our defense
     Secures our safety

                    Salem 09.12.21

*

Conflict Resolution
More like mending fences
Save face
Able to retreat without disgrace
    Than compromise
    And seeing eye to eye
Giving those doubts
    A proper burial
False concepts fall
Not only when pushed
But with the woken dreamer

                Salem 07.30.2020 @2348

*

Frankincense of otherworldliness
I visit from afar
Bringing soil, water and air
Since I could not capture the air
I come to you with
My breath of representation
Having this impact here, wiser
I return home another way

Silver Lake, OR 01.03.21

*

The mind balks
Before it boggles

Salem 06.16.21

*

Trilling down the embarcadero
Take right
On 100 Souls Road
Traveler along the way
Ever rolling
    Never rest
Not a passer-by
    Be blessed
Stop only to help the distressed

        Jerome, ID 08.19.22 @0433

*

There is no see red;
    Redemption
There is only sea red;
    Insatiable appetite

        Salem 09.25.18

*

Trust me
There is a home for it
I will put
    A structure around you
Comfort and protect you
Shelter and amuse you
Your aching head
Tortured heart
There is a home for it
With me

Salem 06.30.20 @1322

Something happened out there
In California
Amongst the waves
Of the deepening ocean
Seaside abodes falling
For its shifting border
Away from the burning acres
Something happened on the streets
Of the projects
Started righting
Writing the wrongs
Something one in the same
Or something very different

Salem 04.02.21

*

There is no simple
Retirement of the facts
Every conclusion
Leads down a certain road

Salem 12.23.19

*

Life is life
Death is death
Troubled by iniquities
When confused on that point
When life imitates death
Or death-life
Authentication then confounding
One is the other

Rockaway Beach, OR 08.28.21

*

Was the west won
Or did it lose it's shooters?
I scrape across the barren desert
I see dry creek beds
Stark playas
Learn their seasonal quench
Acid rain in alkali lakes
To see past my own fraud
Inexplicable miracle
But once done
I had to live a different life

                    Salem 09.11.2020 @0035

*

I was told it was faux gold
I gave it away
So it wouldn't be fools gold
Second guess- my second impression
Realizing scam
Now seeing it foe's gold

                    Salem 09.11.2020 @ 0833

I get the feeling
We are all in
A room running short of oxygen
You do not hold
    Your head down
You do not bother
    To lift

Corvallis, OR 11.20.98

*

Eternal essence of beauty
Ironic for the word
Be it fleeting here
Perhaps not so magical
     As we hoped
Second look at quaking aspen
Exemption by example

          Salem 01.01.19 @1811

*

Premarital hex
Fly too close to the sun
Icarus wax poetic
Pleas old desire
New gravity deaf
Fall, breaks union

Oakridge, OR 12.10.2021

Browning, Poe, Dickinson
Acronym of my fate
Acrimonious if disputed
Initials of my sake
Imbibe yet never reconstituted
Be with me now
Read and ravish allegory

                    Salem   07.25.2020

*

I was sitting by myself
Not within myself

Salem 07.25.2020

*

What was that?
I forethought
The losing of the money clip
Back before Albuquerque
At that time
        I dismissed it as fear
        Loss of a valuable
Now it seems
More premonition
Losing item
        Gaining clairvoyance
Post facto

                    Odessa, Texas 08.21.22 @0222

*

If only
We could discard
Our iniquities to the dirt
It's complex
To my simple mind
In reality, simple in itself
I'm not really sad

Salem 07.25.20

*

We get trapped
In our straight-away visions
Forward facing
First person perspective
Speeding down our roadway
As our sights
     Blurred in the periphery
We collide with each other
En masse

    Deschutes Forest, OR 12.11.21 @ 1219

The sacrificial lamb
The disadvantaged friend
The one whom you feel
    Smarter than
Grammar
The one you feel smarter, then
Every little gram counted
Grammer
Pride suspended alone

Salem 03.07.18

*

Seminole spirit
Fend off opposition
Hope prevailing over termination
Refusing to
      Negotiate our demise
Red Cloud hung over us
Crazy Horse held out
By bone and blood Little Bighorn
It's a third world country
Out there
      Where I have been removed
Place of my abandon
      Where I relinquish
      My reluctance
Now, into the Black Hills

                    Seminole, Texas 08.20.22

*

Invigorated by the ocean
Awoke in its wake
Inevitable I return to land
This time will tide me over

Salem 07.23.20

*

To Love, whole heart
To hate, hole heart
They say there's a
     God-shaped hole
Remaining to fill
Consuming black hole dwarfed
To the celestial whole

                    Salem 06.25.20

*

Lie through teeth
Teeth not a filter
Snarling, biting
Dense, deflecting
Filter through pilgrimage
Highway 90 flushing air
Wind left behind us

                    Albany, OR 01.01.22

*

There are many things
People tend towards
Tend to be selfish
Trend towards populous
Tend towards fear
All disguised
What we pretend to be

Salem 11.28.21

*

Not an impression
It is inclination
That there is something
Undiscovered, more, unknown tell
Of justice
Truth touches all
But does not reside in all

Gilchrist, OR 06.06.21

*

Eddie Ate Dynamite
Good Bye Eddie
Mnemonic guitar playing
Strings to disaster
Minus Eddie

Salem 07.11.19

*

Brisk cold morning
Produced brisk walk
The weather has turned on us
Do not see this
    With cross eyes
Unless it's to then
    See straight culpability
Not only the lambs
But also, bulls
Go to slaughter
Do not hold faith
    In your own will

                          Salem 12.04.18

*

In our relationship
I moved in trust
In slumber
        The breaking of our covenant
Woke me
As a sleeping passenger
Like my spirit moving on
And I awaken in the ride

                Cuba, New Mexico 08.19.22 @1735

*

Is that what this
    Foul-felt fate
    Foreshadows?
Nine out of nine times
I have thoughts of a tenth
Overcast blocks my stars
I gave my heart away
    And there's no return
The void urges
Perpetual spurn
Now relegated to guard

Salem 10.29.17 @0433

*

Crying in the flag
Cling to the rocks on which
The torrent tide torments
In the shallow depths
     Of a deep ocean
Genocide by dilution
My mixed ancestry estranges
I am told to let go
The hand of my ancestor

                    Newport, OR 07.22.19

Euthanasia
More than youth in Asia
We are complicit
Murder of innocents
Murders our innocence

Turn from self-serve tendencies
That divorce within us
When did beauty, joy and comfort
Become not enough?
Never ever enough

Salem 10.01.19

*

You look around here
A place where a many some
Wanted their waning days
Their end sum
The living go to assume
It was ill attributes
Of all this Northwest beauty
Overcast. Fog. Rain.
Ignore Verdancy,
The silver-cast flattering light,
Eyes off the misty mysticism
Divert attention of
        Fresh lung-fulls
Somehow the harmony
Turned discordant
The young turned on the old
They grew old
Then turned on the young
Long addiction
Turned you on yourself

                    Newport, OR 07.22.19

*

What is your relationship
With the eternal?
A footprint
A breath
A particle
A sidenote?
There is a dividing
      Line between

                              Salem 08.01.20

*

While I now walk
As I breathe
I earn your words
Delight in the praise post mortem
That day
When I am gone
When the sun shines down
You know I am there
The chimes in the wind
The brightest star in night

                              Salem 04.03.20

*

Joyous songs
Beats give reference
To past beats
And tail pitched high
Gloomy
Songs that have beats
Disappear, pitched low

Corvallis, OR 10.02.98

*

Life- more often odd
What gives us that impression
More odd than not
That normal defines
Common confines

Salem 10.18.20

*

We are just glass panes
Acting profane
Projectiles passing by
Brink of disaster
Kept intact
They have said it all
Including contradiction
So much more to be said

Christmas Valley, OR 05.09.21

*

God asks of us
Because we can
Accomplish what
     He cannot alone
For He is in us
But is not us
     We are one atoned
Presence can be felt
Not witnessed
Until fulfillment of faith
Eternal rest at home

                    Salem 11.26.17

*

Lessons from the street
See the battles
It is not the most provocative
    Loudest
Definitely not the most popular
Who are victorious

Keizer, OR 04.09.17

*

Deed you well
     And dig it deep
My litany of deeds needs growth
My will as deep as the well
I will wish you well
Bid you well
Well-wish my will perseveres

                    Salem 04.12.22 @1909

*

1000 miles from Albuquerque
In turn
1000 miles from Umatilla Rez
Pushed away
    In the middle
Ultimately pushed out
I walked away
Subsequently lashed out
Against

                Snowville, UT 08.19.22 @0556

*

Annexation of peace
Anticipating
There is evening in the morn

       Salem 09.17.17

*

Wind the second's hand
To push the hours

Corvallis, OR 06.03.99

Euro and buffalo mix
Pair-of-bull, Bi-bull
Makes me bison

                              Salem 04.09.22 @0052

*

The most notorious
     Are still good
By read, not deed
One sided
As negative example to avoid

                    Salem 04.09.22 @1144

*

It is our fate
I see in you
High expectations
In one rendezvous

Corvallis, OR 04.02.99

*

Darkest shadows
Cast by brightest light
Dark, dark
     Foreshadowing

                    Salem 10.15.17

*

Old. Older
Young. Younger
No matter
We are all in the same age
All important
Share matter

Salem 09.30.21

*

Let us first acknowledge
That we are walking wounded
Then seek healing
Over consolation
Praying out in exhausted breath
Crying out in fear of death
Peaked high hopes
Discovered steep slopes
Struggling to connect cause
Damn lusty filth
Fxxx that temptation
Renders me mere meat

Salem 04.27.20

*

Worrisome
The trillion things
That could go wrong
If our creator was chaos

Salem 02.18.19

*

The tolling of the bell
Hear ye, hear ye
Trolling from hell
The death knell
Then the death toll

Salem 05.16.19

*

Feel the gravity stronger
Holding me down
And grounded
    To the
Celestial body
To that, which I am closest
With whom, we share orbit

                    Salem 04.06.22

*

Caught red handed
Blink
I shrink
Back
Yet irreversible

Ute Mountain, Colorado 08.19.22 @1414

*

There are features
That distinguish
     Part of your identity
There are some
     To change
And/or could change
Then there is that piece
I hope you can accept
On way to opus

                              Salem 11.26.17

*

Doubled down on 3
Ended up with 6
Running far from the truth
Down this path
Wonder where truth ever exists
Estranged by distance

Salem 11.16.20

*

Strike a chord
Touch a nerve
Follow my word
It caught up to me
Avoid my shield
Fall on my sword

Albany, OR 06.11.15

*

Every story has its angle
For certain
Every angler has their story

                              Salem 09.11.19

Only way for help
You must escape from here

Navajo Reservation, New Mexico 08.19.22
@1514

*

So lonesome
Any attention
Feels like a serenade
When all else fails
You failed yourself
At your lowest
Depressed basin
You can always
Donate remaining energy
Give yourself away to others
Reversal of fortune

Salem 10.02.18

*

Denying my ancestry
Kills my identity
On my Sioux-side
Where do I belong
Estranged and denied
From vast lands of my past
And immediate blood
      In vein

                    Salem 01.26.21 @1241

*

I am tender
I am weak
Tasting exhaustion
I shall sleep

Corvallis, OR 02.18.99

*

The future flawed
Because it's made of man
Identity made of
Who, what, when, how, why, where
     We are
And that which we wish
     To be
Disgruntled be the man
Acquainted with his dissonant nature

                    Salem 10.16.15

*

E-V'er Junior
That's who they say I was
Followed every song
Before the roaring buzz
E-V'er Junior
I looked up LegalZoom
E-V'er Junior
Met your legal doom
Took a salt bath
Got into your lungs
That which you endured
Pain and anguish stung
Torn limb to limb
Remains soaking rags
Then you left the office
In a yellow
Ledbetter bag

Salem 08.02.21

*

Bird on a wire
Look, a dove above
Peace on the line
Partitioning two sides of sky

      Christmas Valley, OR 12.11.2021

*

Artist brushes
With death
To feel
Alive

Salem 08.16.19

*

Term of art
Nuance vs semantics
Therapy vs creativity
Hypocrisy vs struggle
Pain vs squander
Hapless vs time
Five against versus

Turner, OR 08.08.22

*

Striking out
Against the faceless assailant
Based on one
Damning descriptor
Coloring perspective
Hue are wrong
Hear-say heresy

Salem 06.02.15

*

Could you tell?
Fallen to silence
In the back of this hotel
Lost your heart
And that was your guide

Salem 07.22.15

Prayer powerful
As much the other direction
    In cursing a
    Great name in vain
When bon mot lost on Heaven
One will live like hell

                Salem 05.21.21

*

It is in my fabric
Do not rush me
To be laid out, full view
Convey the lesson
Be the teacher
    Not the lessen-er
To be Pacific in our aim
From red pipestone
Mission in our direction
Conviction come cascading down

        Newport, OR 07.11.20

*

Freedom-
I will die for my life
Salvation-
I will live for my death

Salem 05.06.21

*

In my arms
I felt your muscle twitch
Erratic breathing
As you dreamed in slumber
It was some years back
     That I ground my teeth
In stressed sleep
In that point of hope
I found the point of hope
Last week
     I lamented the week before
The pressure enabled me
To hear my own blood pulsating
Within my ear
My vitality gave rise to the future

                         Salem 11.22.19

*

```
Me
I have not eaten
Amen
I emanate me
Nomen
I emulate no poet
```

                                   Sand Hallow, ID 08.19.22

*

Children at play
Men at work
Women at love

Christmas Valley, OR 10.02.21

*

My nomadic Nakota where-house
Pitched on the prairie
Perched on a ledge
Vibrant on the great plains
Moving on, within

Salem 10.23.19

*

Put an eye on that
Put an "I" on it
This, right here
Not that, over there
You'll put your "I" out

Salem 10.06.21

*

Surreal disorientation
We are upside down
      In our house
What is wrong?
Exigua got your tongue
This life
Ain't what we anticipated

Salem 10.08.21 @0732

*

Sympathize hypocrisy
        As struggle
Rust
Under the paint

                    Corvallis, OR 04.08.99

*

Water and fire mesmerize alike
Bonfire and surf upon the beach
People in boat
Energy undulating underboard
Focused on self, text and tan
Missing life around
Sea lions right outside our wake
     Eating fish
Miss a lot but
That is their reality
They would say life is dry

                    Newport, OR 11.10.19

*

The truth
Is a straight line
Through pale perceptions
And crooked intentions
Despite circular arguments
Denial of existence
Arrow with a point

Salem 06.07.21

*

Best summarized
Verbatim

Corvallis, OR 05.09.99

*

If not obstinate
Perhaps they were musicians
Maybe poets
Told them to refrain
And they continued
To do it repeatedly

Salem 02.24.19

*

Revenge, fugitive, resentment
Have no place here
Where our enduring closeness
Dulcet affections
Confections of love
Dominate in our domicile
Former dichotomy
Treasonous as we are adjoined
Take bow now
    For eternity

Salem 11.03.19

*

Blackest black
Noir tres noir
Negro intenso
Permian Basin
Underground ocean
Powering the surface
In turn
        Burns into the atomos

                    Amarillo, TX 08.22.22 2355

*

It started
79 Jupiter red eye flight
Search far and wide
Your fingerprints
Like a topographic map
No treasure marked
Perhaps the fountain
    Of youth
Is more like
    Eutrophication

                          Salem 08.18.22 @0921

*

I call their bluff
I call them out
It all ends
    When I call their name

                    Salem 02.20.21

*

Life with Brad
Arbiter of truth
In all hope
Hope sometimes reality
Bromides vs Bona Fides

Christmas Valley, OR 05.20.22 @0021

*

Aging Vitruvian man
Measurement by
Earth, Heaven and hell
Circle triangle square
Attempts to elevate
The spacecraft shot
     Into the stratosphere
Unexpectedly exploding
Continued into the heavens

                Salem 03.08.19 @0322

*

Live to feed self
Net zero

Live a gross life
Return to the fallow ground
Need to deprive
Yourself
To rebuild good hunger

Salem 03.08.19 @1217

*

Walking under rainbows
Swimming past
     Ever-living hydras
Tasting raspberries
     From the center
     Of the universe
Why listen
To simpleton celebrities
1000 mile stare the wrong way
Take real long view
Give me some more, give me
Some more,
     Give me some more oh

                    Salem 06.09.20

*

The severed limbs
Of the mighty oak
Have not
The numerous rings
As the trunk

Castle Rock, CO 08.24.22 @1059

*

Led into battle
For my country
Old Glory
    Wrap my wounds
Yankton Flag
    Tourniquet

                Salem 06.02.22

You pigeon-holed yourself
To the hawks
We have superpowers
As humans
We take for granted
Flagrant ways self-serving
To the point
    You lose all meaning
No way to have yourself
    Guaranteed eternity on earth
May try with publication
Progeny wanting substantiation
That others carry on your name

    Christmas Valley, OR 03.11.21

*

Father, son, husband, Holy Ghost
Running through the hail
    Pelting my coat
Tears stream out
Without a cry
Passer-by without an alibi
Those who know me not
Try to define
Now I caught the clarity
Not despite
But through the pain
    Transforming energy
    Fourth rendition
    Giving inspiration
Pulling you along for the ride

        Portland, OR 06.06.22

*

White light
Full spectrum
Demonized for shadow cast
Not everything; your cost
Could be a Pentecost
Not everything you lose
     Is a loss

Salem 03.11.21 @1104

*

We deride though
We are the deviants
Act of God or governor?
Lies swilling
Fires burning
Swirling smoke suffocating
Just give me one good reason

Salem 09.18.20

*

"Better than nothing"
Superior as something
Or
Inferior to all
Black hole
Superstar in density
Substellar in light

Ute Mountain Reservation, CO 08.19.22

*

The system confounded
Then restricted us
We decidedly fought,
     Pushed against
When the lid snapped tight
We adjusted to fit
Into the spaces between us
We then realigned priority
To where we've been wronged
Off right

                    Salem 07.29.20 @0308

*

As I stand
Right here
Feel my fate
Objectified by my surround
Rickety sun bleached burnt out barn
Scars on it
Epitaph writ
I should go, not to own
My sum lessened in this aggregate
As I go
Change of fate

Echo, OR 08.18.22 @2246

*

We are all going
The same direction
It is a certain tide
Before we know it
It is over
Trend vanquished
That is RIP tide
Blind as in prosperity
Deaf as an all-star celebrity
No, the most of us shall push
Against and press forward
Work to fix
  Everything always breaking
Exasperated and traumatized
Yes, press on
Heartily

       Salem 05.27.22

*

Opt in
Or
Opt out
It is our special position
Opt ion

Salem 11.21.21 @2304

*

Focus on the road
Memories indistinct
Watching the end horizon
Distinctive road,
Peripheral blurred
Dedication to truth
    Makes for steadfastness
You do
Or you do not
Gatekeeper

                    Gilchrist, OR 11.29.20

*

Not deserving of a burn down
We all have dead branches
On a living tree
Funeral pyre
Much more than an effigy

Salem 12.06.17

*

Worldly things wrought
     From Heaven
Perplexing, Heaven moves
Not worldly
     Antithesis of Heaven
How our celestial particulate
Yearn for above
Away from this
How we confuse worship
     Of worldly things
As celestial endeavor
Mistaken as Heavenly
Nothing inevitable
Two sparks akin
Conjoined inextricably
One a flash, one perpetual

Salem 06.01.19

*

I am the kind of rare breed
Rarity that could
Love you forever
The hit and the sober
The hit and the classic
The hit and the defense
The hit and the tackle

Christmas Valley, OR 12.31.20

Edge of disaster
Precipice of faith

Salem 12.26.20 @1735

*

Desert stripped us
Of our defenses
And our iniquities
We had to provide to our thirst
No peace in the sedate mind
Some set out on a search
You sojourned away from faith
What developments
Have you realized
Nada, only anti-material
There is no alternate Truth
    To discover
Only facets of the One

                    Salem 02.20.21

*

Various wounds
Can be mortal
If let-left to fester

                    Salem 06.17.22 @0007

*

I get paid accolades
For which I do not
Have pockets

                        Corvallis, OR 03.05.99

*

You have a list of names
      On a page
The darkness of the harm
If I gave you my list
      On that page
It would blot it all out black

                              Salem 07.31.20

*

Incomplete control
Good by word
Not by deed

Salem 09.13.22 @1054

*

A condition
Defines the stagnant
Publishing would solidify
     The identity
For those wanting change
     Will grow
     And use that
     As a point of no return

Christmas Valley, OR 10.02.21 @1354

*

The good word rained down
I sheltered against it
Not accepted as a river
    Water carving a channel
    Flowing life internally
Not as an underground aqueduct
    Quenching the desert
Not as a cleansing shower
No- I deflected with roof
But then reflected with proof
If not mist
Cold dawning

Salem 08.23.20

*

No matter what it was
Or was not
We were meant to
Be there that time
He was meant to
Say it in that way
We were meant to
Hear it that way
You were meant to
Inquire about it
And we were better
     For it
Now it worked out
     Better this way

Salem 09.11.22 @1556

*

The cool water cold
Traveling over the mountains
To the streams
And now to me
That water warms in hand
Now warm water
Now the same family

Christmas Valley, OR 03.21.21 @1029

*

I did not go there
For the education
Not there
I came there for
The increase
Of one degree

Salem 07.29.20 @1346

The wind is in my favor
The tide is not
The light tilts favorably
The heat, caught in a pot
Building a boiling
Shaking and quaking
Pressure, pressure!
Pressure, pressure!
Made the food
Now I'm fed, led to bed

Salem 07.15.21

*

The beginning of the rainbow
Is light
Suspended droplets
The body is rain

Leaves you
Elusive end of the rainbow
Tales of treasure, unfulfilled
Trails between sunray and moonbeam
Prism, out of angles

Pleasant Hill, OR 05.19.22 @2006

*

Find a creature foreign
Look at those eyes
They are not eyes
They can not-see
Sightless eyespots
Shaken my core
Step back
Not sure
    Of what is navigating

Salem 09.15.21 @0729

*

Intently inhale
The fresh air
Deeper than as you had
The smoke

     Gilchrist, OR 08.22.21 @1255

*

*

Awards and Honors

- October through November 2022- Singular Award, Imitating Imitation Writing Contest; Writer's Café (Of Something Great, Cantus, 2010). Cogito Group; Presented by Swagato Saha

- October through November 2022- Particular Award, Imitating Imitation Writing Contest; Writer's Café (Ability Falls to Will, Cantus, 2010). Cogito Group; Presented by Swagato Saha

- March 2015 — Hero Award, Salem Health; Salem Hospital ICU Medical Social Worker

- January 2015 — Hero Award, Salem Health; Salem Hospital ICU Medical Social Worker

- December 2014 — Team Award, Salem Health; Salem Hospital ICU Medical Social Worker

Shadow Catcher
Syzzer
Cornflake
Palaka
B Dizzle
D Train
The Voice
Big Baby
Paco
Chief Iron Stomach
Hatchet Man
Bravo Papa Delta
Chopper
Cali
Brine
Big Hungry
Conan

*

*

*

- *Shadow Catching: Poems of Existential Peering (2022)*
- *Syzygy: Poems of Essential Theory (2020)*
- *Dose: Poems of Quintessential Ethereality (2016)*
- *Cantus: A Book of Poems (2010)*

Cantus: A Book of Poems
Paperback ISBN-13: 978-0-982-9733-0-1 & ISBN-10: 0-982-97330-6
Hardcover ISBN: 978-0-9829733-3-2
http://www.amazon.com/Cantus-Brad-Dehler/dp/0982973306/

Dose: Poems of Quintessential Ethereality
Paperback ISBN-13: 978-0-982-9733-1-8 & ISBN-10: 0-982-97331-4
Hardcover ISBN: 978-0-9829733-4-9
https://www.amazon.com/Dose-Quintessential-Ethereality-Brad-Dehler/dp/0982973314

Syzygy: Poems of Essential Theory
Paperback ISBN-13: 978-0-982-9733-2-5 & ISBN-10: 0-982-97332-2
Hardcover ISBN: 978-0-9829733-5-6
https://www.amazon.com/Syzygy-Essential-Theory-Brad-Dehler/dp/0982973322

*

*

www.ingramcontent.com/pod-product-compliance
Lightning Source LLC
Chambersburg PA
CBHW070938130626
46555CB00001B/487